REBECA I. STRONG

Great Money Adventures

— Penny —

GREAT MONEY ADVENTURES
PENNY

iUniverse books may be ordered through booksellers or by contacting:

iUniverse
1663 Liberty Drive
Bloomington, IN 47403
www.iuniverse.com
1-800-Authors (1-800-288-4677)

ISBN: 978-1-5320-4298-0 (sc)
ISBN: 978-1-5320-4299-7 (e)

Library of Congress Control Number: 2018909173

Print information available on the last page.

iUniverse rev. date: 10/18/2018

To my children, Jared and Ethan Strong. Thank you
for your love and patience. You are my inspiration
and motivation. Mommy loves you so much!

Special Thanks

Thank you, Lord, for all you give us. Thank you
for friends, family, and all the beauty around us.

Notes to Parents and Teachers

This book is designed as an aid to help preschool children learn how to count to ten and recognize and learn the value of a penny. This book is a great way to introduce the penny, as the children will have the opportunity to ponder some open-ended questions, such as the following: What does the head of the penny look like? What color is it? What do you see? This book is a fun, interactive way to learn, as it's intended to expand children's creativity and understanding of the world around them. They will sing and dance their way into learning. It would be helpful to allow the children to hold and admire a real penny before and/or after reading this book. This book also features true animals and flowers found around the world.

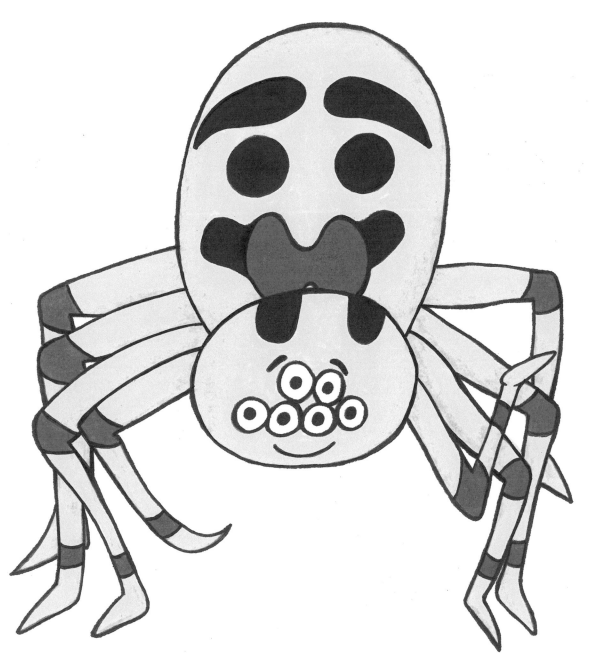

This is a happy-face spider. His name is Kaholo. He has a very important job to do! He is the keeper of this book, and all the animals in this book pay him pennies for what they want to do.

A penny is one of the many forms of money.

 = 1¢

Kaholo would like to show you what a penny looks like.

This is the front of the penny; also called the head of the penny.

This is the back of the penny; also called the tail of the penny.

What shape is the penny? What color is it? Do you see a picture in the penny?
What else do you see?

We pay money to enjoy things or buy things we need. Can you think of things you need money for?

Today is Activity Fun Day, and Kaholo the spider must now go out and work. Today he will be giving out prize pennies to the animals who earn them by the activities they complete. Each activity completed will earn them a penny. Can you help Kaholo count all the pennies?

This is Squirms the worm. His activity of choice is making numbers using only his body. Can you help point and count?

Squirms can't figure out how to do the number 10! He completed 9 numbers.

How many pennies did Squirms earn if he completed 9 numbers? Great job!

Kaholo owes Squirms the worm 9 pennies for completing 9 numbers!

= 9¢

This is Bumble the rusty-patched bumblebee. He would like to play in the exotic flowers. How many flowers does Bumble play in? Can you point and count?

Fireman 1

Artist 2

Dancer 3

Biologist 4

Doctor 5

Police Officer 6

Astronaut 7

Fantastic! Bumble played with 7 flowers.

How many pennies does Kaholo the spider owe Bumble for playing in 7 exotic flowers?

Good job!

Kaholo the spider owes Bumble 7 pennies!

= 7¢

Hey, Bori! Bori is a coqui. His activity of choice is singing. Bori will sing as many songs as he knows. Can you help count how many songs he knows?

Coqui, coqui, coqui, coqui!

Yay! Everyone Clap for Bori! Do you know any other songs Bori? Yes? OK. Sing us another song.

Coqui, coqui, coqui, coqui!

Hey, Bori, that is the same song. Do you know another? No? OK. Bori only knows one song.

How many pennies does Kaholo owe Bori for his one song? You are so smart! Yes. Kaholo owes Bori one penny for his one song. Outstanding!

 = 1¢

Rocco is a coral snake. His activity of choice is making shapes with his body. Can you count how many shapes he can make with his body?

Triangle 1

Circle 2

Heart 3

Rectangle 4

Diamond 5

star 6

Oval 7

Square 8

How many shapes did Rocco complete? That's right! He completed 8!

If Rocco completed 8 shapes, then how many pennies does Kaholo owe Rocco?

Yes! Kaholo owes Rocco 8 pennies

= 8¢

Hey there! This is Alli the alligator. Her activity of choice is to see how many of her babies will be hatching today. Can you point and count?

There is 1! That's Mater the gator!

And 2! That's Vader the gator!

And 3! That's Slater the gator! Maybe the rest will hatch later.

Alli is the proud mommy of three today. How many pennies does Kaholo owe Alli the gator?

Of course, Kaholo owes Alli 3 pennies for 3 babies. Outstanding!

   = 3¢

Well, hello there, Ronaldo! He is a dart frog. Ronaldo is an athlete and he plays sports. How many sports does Ronaldo play?

Basketball 1

Hockey 2

Soccer 3

Baseball 4

Ronaldo plays four different sports. Amazing, Ronaldo! How many pennies does Kaholo owe him for playing four different sports? Yes. Kaholo owes him 4 pennies. Terrific job!

= 4¢

Kai the fly wants to dance today. He will dance to as many songs as he can without getting tired. Can you help? He needs a song to dance to. Can you sing and dance to the ABCs? Ready?

ABCDEFGHIJKLMNOPQRSTUVWXYZ
Now I know my ABCs, next time won't you sing with me?

Yay! Now we need another song. Can you help again? Can you sing and dance to "The Itsy Bitsy Spider"? Ready? 1, 2, 3!

The itsy bitsy spider went up the water spout. Down came the rain and washed the spider out. Out came the sun and dried up all the rain, and the itsy bitsy spider went up the spout again!

Great moves, everyone! Lovely singing!

Kai the fly danced to 2 songs today. How many pennies does Kaholo owe Kai? That's right! He gets 2 pennies for 2 songs.

 = 2¢

Hello, Thiago! Thiago is a red-eyed tree frog! His activity of choice is to jump up high to see what adventures await.

How many adventures does Thiago have? Can you point and count?

10

Thiago had 10 adventures! How many pennies does Kaholo
owe Thiago? Thiago gets 10 pennies. Excellent!

= 10¢

You are amazing!

Thank you for playing, and singing with us today. It was fun helping Kaholo count pennies. We had a great time. You were such a great helper and we would like to invite you to come play with us again on other adventures. See you later, alligator!

Printed in the United States
By Bookmasters